THE REBIRTH OF SPOKEN WORD

HERU SENGHOR FATIU

The Rebirth of
Spoken Word

The Rebirth of
Spoken Word

Heru Senghor Fatiu a.k.a. Hannibal

authorHOUSE®

AuthorHouse™
1663 Liberty Drive
Bloomington, IN 47403
www.authorhouse.com
Phone: 1-800-839-8640

First published by AuthorHouse   07/26/2011

ISBN: 978-1-4634-2456-5 (sc)
ISBN: 978-1-4634-2457-2 (ebk)

Library of Congress Control Number: 2011910009

Printed in the United States of America

Contents

Acknowledgments

I owe thanks to a lot of people for inspiring me to write this book of poetry. I thank the Creator and the Ancestors first and foremost for allowing me to come out of the darkness of ignorance and into the light of self knowledge. Without this newfound love and knowledge of self this book wouldn't be possible. I have to give a huge thank you to Brother Kitau, the father who nurtured me as if I was his biological son when I was a young teenager trapped in the belly of the beast. I have to thank the Collective Thinkers who helped develop my consciousness when I was a P.O.W. in the so-called Correctional Facilities. I have to think my new family the Fatiu's for continuing to further develop my consciousness now that I have been released into a larger prison called "society". I'd like to thank my mother, Bernadette Sample and my father, John Walker. God bless their souls for being the vessels the Creator chose to bring me into this world. And I would be remiss if I didn't mention the special appreciation I have for my future wife Melita Smith who sacrificed her time to help me transcribe all my pieces. You are a beautiful woman and a precious gift who I really adore. I have to acknowledge my beautiful children Amaya, Ma'at and Naasir who constantly inspire me to write and fight for their future. I love and respect all the following people: Edena, Elo a.k.a. Imhotep 7, Taharka, Lumumba, Knowledge Ra, Muhammad, Jimmy Djewhety, Gamba, Black, Sam R.I.P., Aba Hotep, Sunshine and Nazeen. Each one of you played a pivotal role in my development and supported me throughout my incarceration. Another thank you goes out to my brother, Heru a.k.a. FreedomWriter for assisting me in the second printing of this book. And I have to give a special shout-out to Brother Asis for constantly encouraging me to put my best foot forward and for helping me to put my book together. I thank you brother, you are appreciated and loved. For all those who directly had an impact in my life that I failed to mention. I love and appreciate all of your contributions as well.

I dedicate this book to all of you.

Authors Note

I was in prison when I first became culturally and politically conscious of our oppression as a people; consequently it explained a lot of my constant disappointments, failures, hurt and rage in my life. I was incarcerated at the age of sixteen for murder and I was sentenced to fifteen years in prison and I served ten years, two months and sixteen days before I was released back into the larger prison commonly referred to as society. Before I was incarcerated I could barely read or write and I was thoroughly convinced (thanks to the Baltimore City public school system and this white supremacist society) that I was incapable of achieving any academic success. It wasn't until brothers began to introduce me to our people's history that I began to grow and believe in my natural human potential to achieve any objective I set for myself. I learned a lot over the years about our history and political struggle as an African people and my poetry reflects my development.

When I wrote my first poem I didn't recognize my work as poetry. I was eighteen years old and on lock-up at ECI (a prison system in the state of Maryland). I read my work to a 5% brother on lock-up with me and he yelled back down the tier "that's poetry!" I told him that it was just an expression of my thoughts. I didn't agree with people labeling my work as poetry then because the only poetry I heard of at the time was for entertainment purposes only. I wasn't expounding Revolutionary Thoughts to entertain, I was writing poetry to educate and uplift a fallen people. It wasn't until later after I was exposed to other people who wrote poetry for the purpose of liberating the shackled minds of our people that I began to embrace the title of Poet. A poet, to me, is a person who expounds beautiful words of liberation that deliver strength, faith, direction, endurance, knowledge, courage, wisdom, understanding and love to the ears of their listeners.

Art is beautiful only when it has a meaningful purpose. Kemet (the original name of Egypt) was one of our greatest societies. The entire nation of Kemet was a work of art with meaning and purpose woven throughout. From Heru-Em-Akhet (The Sphinx) to the Tekenu (obelisks), we learn lessons about taming the beast within and remembering the interconnectedness between heaven and earth through these great works of art. Our art today has to match the art of Kemet in helping us to realize our maximum potential as human beings.

I pray that my humble revolutionary thoughts can deliver some strength, faith, direction, endurance, knowledge, courage, wisdom, understanding and love to the ears of those who choose to listen so more of our people will begin to realize that we too can reach our maximum potential as human beings. Thank you for your support.

Your beloved brother in the struggle,
Heru Senghor Fatiu

Introduction

History informs us that at a certain point in time there always emerges men and women of exceptional character. Women and men destined to make an indelible impression upon the world and alter the course of history. History itself attests to this! Men and women are made by history and likewise women and men make history. Its a dialectical relationship.

Brother Heru is, at once, making and being made by history with the publication of his collection of passionate and personal poems. Emotionally charged, raw and uncut, "The Rebirth of Spoken Word" is a must read for all who appreciate art and creativity. From the onset with "Talking About Revolution" all the way through to "Come Back To Reality", Brother Heru is speaking from his soul to the souls of Afriken people.

"My Pain" is raw and personal to the core. Within this poem, the author captures so poetically, the pain and frustration engendered within him while incarcerated. Neither ashamed nor embarrassed by this episode within his life, Brother Heru honestly and passionately shares with us those internal and infernal feelings and emotions bred within him by the prison system. He opted to vent and channel these emotions through poetry. Not just any type of poetry, but poetry to feed the souls and nourish the minds of his people: Afriken people.

"The Rebirth of Spoken Word" is a mission statement; a poetic call to action and Brother Heru emerges from its pages as a liberator, a freedom fighter. "P.O.W.", "My Father Died" and "Destruction of Black Civilization" all attest to his passion and commitment to the redemption, reformation and restoration of his people. This becomes apparent from reading the first poem "Untitled".

Throughout the book, Brother Heru writes of freedom, liberation, revolution, praise, reverence, dignity, respect and love (for and of his people). From start to finish he writes, consistently, to and about his people. Reminding us in "The Things We Forgot" of our achievements, contributions to Humanity and obligation to restore. Brother Heru has managed to compose a poignant and compelling piece of work. This masterful collection of poetry holds no punches. Its blunt, forceful and straight to the point.

Imhotep Asis Fatiu

Untitled

A Slave to industry like the Scare Crow in The Wizard of Oz

Share-croppers locked down behind steel bars

How can I compete with automation?

A computerized Nation has made Man Obsolete

In 2073 we all will be hungry and out on the streets

Except for a few Cyborg elite

T Ford Model 9 snatching souls online

The science of cybernetics is secretly being instilled into our genetics

The spreading of A.I.D.S.

Is to make way for the clones and drones

And is the same reason why ET phoned home

They want to be left alone to destroy the planet

I look up to Nana Nyame and I know y'all Niggas don't understand me because

y'all too caught up in the schism of Islam and Christianity while we are faced with

the end of Hue-manity

They possess the technology of the Greys

And pretty soon they are going to blast us with their plasma rays

Stay out of the beast if you don't want to be found

X-Men with out super powers hide underground

The final phase of Star Wars initiated the intergalactic battle for the

Colonization of space

Have aliens walking around on Mars with the Gas Face

The purpose of science fiction is to make us believe that the invasion of aliens is

Fictitiously conceived

Remember the Invasion of the Body Snatchers?

When they abducted our Ancestors into the hulls of their ships

And programmed us to hate our God, Culture and physical characteristics

We never been the same

Some of us have managed to take the chips out of our brains

But be careful who you trust

Because although he looks like me and acts like me underneath his mask

He just might be a V

I see everything but I don't allow everything to see me

Because the Olympians are 7 feet tall and ride on Chariots of fire

One glance from them will evaporate your soul

The only thing that they are interested in is silver and gold

And the destruction of your cosmic Ba

I seek refuge in Ptah

Universal Soldiers deployed

Got the community paranoid

Women stressed

Male babies snatched from their breast

There's only a few of us left

And Big Brother is watching

Secretly plotting our demise

I refuse to be vaporized

The system has to die

Fire in my eyes

A reflection of my soul

Violence in the streets explode

Man against Machine

We can only win this battle in our dreams

The Resistance is losing focus

The masses are beginning to believe that freedom is hopeless

A few weary souls march on and had the enemy alarmed

We finally realize we cant beat the system with tanks and bombs

So we secretly log on

To the Mainframe

And inject a computer virus into The Brain

Everything came to a stand still and the people began to distinguish the fake from the real

Technology collapsed

And the system was driven back

Until it disintegrated

Everyone was elated and Freedom was celebrated

Revolution! Created by: Heru Senghor

Talking About Revolution

The sky is gray and the moon is crying

The sound of soldiers foot steps marching through the Ghetto streets of America

The trumpets are resounding

And its past the eleven fifty five hour

The earth is shaken

And the Negro has awakened

With blood in His eye

Pain in his chest

AK47 and a body armored vest

The season has changed from the prosperity of spring

To the fall of America and its corruptible dream

Jaga warriors screammm!!!

Grenades are no longer in our eyes

They are in our hands

Buildings collapse

Plastic explosives concealed in African head wraps

Militarily equipped

With unseen warships

Loose lips is the only thing that can sink our ships

Anthrax is in the air

Bodies are falling everywhere

And we are talking about Revolution

The time is now, our future is at stake

Sound the trumpet the dead must awake

Harriet Tubman said that we are entitled to two things

Liberty or Death

And she was talking about Revolution

Coming through the darkness of night like the Underground Railroad

Guided by the talking drum

Bump! Bump! Bump! Bump!

Suddenly silence . . .

They thought it was over until we climbed over their barricades

And dismembered them in a fit of rage and violence

Savagely they screammm!!!

We surrender to you mighty African warriors . . .

Last of the great Sun Kings

But their pleas fell on deaf ears

Their worst fears have manifested

The red, black and green

Replaced the Star Spangled banner and the American Dream

The statue of slavery cried

Because we killed the great Harlot and raised the flag of Ma'at into the sky

Revolution prevailed

And we hummed the chant of Cetewayo

Zulu! Zulu! Zulu!

And we was talking about the Revolution

The time is now

Our future is at stake

Sound the trumpet

The dead must awake

Cetewayo said

That the white man had until dawn to clear our land

And he was talking about Revolution, And he was talking about Revolution

Revolution! Created by: Heru Senghor

My Father Died

Life has short-changed me in every single area

Life is like a horror movie

A nightmare that never ends

No, I do not need to talk to the Islamic coordinator or the Christian Chaplain

They are the reason why this nightmare is happening

I wish we would have killed them on sight

No more being passive or talking in symbols

All the revolutionary rhetoric just went out the window

My father died

But he never was alive

That's why I shed no tears

But my anger increased

Another young promising Black man destroyed by the Towering Beast

When will the pain cease

I am ready to kill them back

I am not trying to please the few

Because I represent the many

I am more than three-fifths of a man

I am 100% Alkebulan

I know the Negroes don't understand what I am saying

But I am ready to put them on the back burners too

I am down with all slaves to the back

The Negroes, Coons and Afro-Americans holding us back

Are about to get trampled on

I am in agreement with Roy Ayers

Where's our freedom song?

We been marching for too damn long

Stand up and be strong

Lets act instead of react

Strategize and attack

We are dying anyway

We are dying anyway

We might as well fight for our survival

Put down their Holy books and pick up our African spiritual revivals

We are African Nations

Beautiful generations

Reduced to tribalism

Fratricide

Genocide

No where you can run

No where you can hide

Pick up the gun and follow the sun

Become the chosen one of Amen

My father died

Full blown A.I.D.S. was the main killer that took him to the grave

What the hell is a green monkey?

And how did he make his way from Africa across the globe

This is how they say this epidemic explodes

But watch how their diabolical scheme unfolds

Fort Detrick Maryland is where they planed our demise

WHO was steering and directing this scheme?

The World Health Organization for those who don't know what that means

I guess they concocted that story about the velvet monkey

Because they thought we was green

Couldn't comprehend the genetically engineered mixture of

Hepatitis B and Small Pox vaccines

Mad scientists passing off as medical doctors

Initiating Biological Chemical Warfare on the Black masses

Like the triangular slave trade when we were destroyed for Blackstrap Molasses

If you cant see what I am saying I suggest you purchase glasses

Pick up a book and study your self

Learn about your inherited wealth

Solutions are better than resolutions

Stop inhaling America's pollution

Grab the bull by the horns

Like they grabbed the Blackman by his groin

Eviscerate

Emasculate

White Supremacy sealed my father's fate

That's why my heart continues to ache

How much more of this will the African Nation take?

My father died

And like Brother Kitau

No more tears shall I cry

Revolution! Created by: Heru Senghor

A Leader Is What We Need

A leader is what we need

So they say

But every where I look I see a so-called leader standing on a ghetto throne

Shouting loud enough for all to hear

That we no longer need to live in fear

That we are the chosen people of Jesus

Allah

And all the rest of the gods

As one of his disciples shout out "Preach Hard!"

The people see him standing firm and trimmed in gold

After his galvanizing speech the crowd explodes

Laughing

Crying

Shouting out our so called leaders name

As he reaches the peak of his manipulative game

"I need money to bring this about . . ."

The leader shouts

This is the part I don't understand

Why cant they see the contradiction in this devilish man

You don't find it funny

That he needs money

When he lives in the land of milk and honey

Compared to my domain

Which is surrounded by hunger and pain

He rides in limos and on jet planes

Telling me stories of his world glory

How we have friends all across the globe

But not one of them has heard my cries

Or came to the funeral when my Brother died

You didn't even come, so-called leader

Didn't bother to answer any of my letters either

A leader is what we need, so they say

But every where I look I see so called leaders standing on ghetto thrones

Marching in front of Texaco

And all across America begging for jobs

Kneeling on their knees and praying to false gods

They been kneeling on their knees so long that their backs have become bent

Always wanting to rent

Never wanting to own

And then wonder why we don't have a home

Still singing that played-out song

We shall overcome without doing the White Devils any harm

How are you going to overcome without picking up a gun?

This white devil has bombs

And all kinds of military arms

I am not scared to die so-called leader

And I hope that you're not either

The revolution will go on with or without you

We don't want integration

We want separate states to call our own

If you don't want that so-called leader we are sitting you down

Because you're a fake

A con man, A puppet, A fraud

And the only thing that you are good for is preaching hard

Revolution! Created by: Heru Senghor

A Young Black Prisoner

A young Black prisoner lost and confused

another poor victim caught in the White man's ruse

Why do I use the term the white man's ruse? Because he's the main

reason why we are lost and confused

Dirty white cracker devil ought to be a shame, talking about waging

a war on drugs when he's the king of the game

Trying to devour the young Black prisoner with his trickery and flames

Playing us one against the other inundating our communities

with guns and drugs so we can kill each other

A young Black prisoner lost and confused another poor victim

caught up in the White man's ruse

Why cant you see the pain? The young Black prisoner feels trapped in

perdition for keeping it real

Who among you can justifiably say the young Black prisoner was

wrong? Were you ever raised up in the midst of Vietnam?

You bourgeoisie Negroes talking about toughening up integration and laws on crime, don't you know that your aiding and abetting the White man's crimes?

A young Black prisoner lost and confused another poor victim

caught up in the White man's ruse

Today every Black person talking about revolution and change, but

they are perpetuating the White man's institutions with their American names

How can you renounce the enemy and still carry his name?

A young Black prisoner lost and confused another poor victim

caught up in the White man's ruse

Everybody is going to pay when the young Black prisoner

awakens from his sleep

Graves will be dug for the masters of deception,

the psychopathic bastards will finally pay for their crimes

For the years and years of the psychological indoctrination of

the young Black prisoners mind.

Revolution! Created by: Heru Senghor

P.O.W.

The administration is watching our every move

But they are to blind to see

That the revolution is coming

And its coming through me

They locked up our leaders

But their minds are still free

Incarceration is another form of slavery

Our ancestors fought too hard for us to continue the legacy of a slave

We owe them the honor of fighting for freedom until we join them in the grave

I fight while I am behind the steel

With information

Trying to bring the population education

Castration

Is what we are facing

For standing up like men

How can we win?

When the outside world wont intervene in our struggle

They juggle

With our lives

Contrive

Pernicious plans

To strangle the inner voice

Get rid of any one who they consider a powerful force

Lets come together with a revolutionary mentality

To get this prison to manifest an African reality

What will it take?

To awake the sleeping minds of MCI-H

We cant continue to let the Devil control our fate

These brick walls cant stall

Our mental or physical growth

I hope

To one day hang these crackers by the rope

Pressure is thick

And it tends to burst pipes

But it makes me want to fight

We have to do this thing right

Get rid of the rioters mentality

Because it only produces fatalities

I know you want to see blood

Because your part revolutionary and part thug

But first lets grow in numbers

Before we are blown asunder

Sometime you have to go under

Deep under

Ground

So your ideas can't be found

By the enemy

We all are targets

So we have to duck

To continue our plight

Shine our light

On the masses

How can we let **ASSES**

Outthink Alkebulan's finest?

Even if they are standing right in front of us

They shouldn't be able to find us

This is the penal

The Black mans battling ground

We have to be profound

To tear these brick walls down

And put an end to the revolving door

This is our war

You outside whores

That leave us to die

Won't even try

To aid our struggle

Tricked by their propaganda

Murderous slander

Of the convict

It makes me sick

That we are in here suffering and Nigga's ain't even doing shit

If you're lucky enough to get this information in your hand

Blackman

Blackwoman

Become a voice

For those whose voice is being suppressed

By the Grand Dragon

This is not a game

Share my pain

I might not never make it back to the streets

But you can't say that I was weak

Because I continue to speak out against the injustice

Protest it

Protest it

Protest it

The **P.O.W.**

Revolution! Created by: Heru Senghor

Empty Speech

Professing to be God body

But that's all you do is break down bodies

Using your tongue as a twelve gauge shotty

Spitting words of corruption

Stagnating minds with your snake like tongue

Head so BIG with pride

That you can't even see that your brain has been fried

Agent provocateur

Whore

For Willie Lynch's plan

Of perpetual separation

Mr. Black Bruce Banner

Say the wrong words to you in the wrong manner

And watch you burst out of your clothes

I mean . . .

Out of your disguise

Emotions never lie

I can see the hate in your eyes

Snake charmer

Rocking brothers to sleep

With your hypnotic words

But your actions are absurd

Yeah, you're god backwards

Trying to feed off of our dry bones

Mentally en-caged animal

You cant pull a fast one over on Hannibal

Because I've seen your kind

Time and time again

Talking about we should be men

While secretly you commit sin

Unrighteous deeds

I have love for the blind

But I cant continue to allow them to manipulate promising minds

85er

10%

Savage

Cabbage head

Mentally dead

I fear none

Not even Ra

Isfet is a crime

Punishable by death

Save your breath

If you cant formulate the words of MDW NTR

Its better to remain silent

Your actions are violent

Like the devil you proclaim to hate

Mentally we've been raped

And scarred

Walking around like we are actually manifesting the attributes

Of the Creator

Be aware of imitators

Slick-talkers, Bullshit walkers

Holier than thou authors

Pointing the accusatory finger

For minor misdemeanors

Trying to keep us apart

Jealousy and envy breeds in their heart

Everybody can't be saved

So we have to keep the zombies in their graves

Because they feed on brains

Like Dracula and his long fangs

Sucking the blood out of our veins

Mentally we are being drained

So cover your ears

When these empty talkers come near

This is how we will persevere

Ptahhotep teaches us to pay no attention to his evil speech

He's nothing but a leech

Our self control

Will expose

His empty Ba

Everybody begotten by Ra is not of Amon-Ra

Revolution! Created by: Heru Senghor

Where Am I At?

Where am I at?

Streets filled with liquor bottles

Syringes

And rats

Little sisters pregnant

Wondering where their baby's fathers are at

Grown men living with their mothers . . .

And beating on their lovers

Brothers

Beefing over a corner that belong to the Chinese

Sister crawling on her knees

To freeze her reality

Broken homes

Children left on their own

Six year old sister thinks she grown

Elders moan

And then pick up the telephone

Cop killed kid in front of Mr. Wilson home

Legislation passed

To get rid of the vile and wild

Depopulating the community

By kidnapping the fatherless child

Politicians smile

At the blind faith of the community

Brothers and Sisters think that they are immune to H.I.V.

A.I.D.S.

Infests

The neighborhood

And cut us down like a double-edged sword

Do you still want the player of the year award?

Where am I at?

Schools are ill-equipped to handle the children that attend

They rather pass them to the next grade than deal with them again

Ministers preaching about sin

The downfall of men

But never getting actively involved

Make a lot of noise over the podium while their community steadily dissolves

Into Sodom and Gomorra

Cops wage war on drugs

Label all Blackmen as Thugs

Black woman get no respect

Only seen as an object for sex

Only means of support is a welfare check

Cycle of Black on Black violence

Hate

And crime

15 story buildings that en-cage the mind

Open 24 hours a day mortuary signs

Everything is in a state of decline

Moving so fast that we don't have time to live

The only time we have is to bury our dead

Where the fuck you think I am at!

The Ghetto

Revolution! Created by: Heru Senghor

Innocence Lost Part II

Where's her glory?

The same old story

About a innocent young girl

Age seventeen

Who grew up on the streets

With no love

Guidance

Or understanding

In a world of perpetual corruption

Her mind was stolen

By alien abduction

Chemical substance

Trapped in Charlotte's Web

By some Bitch that goes for bad

Attitude shitty

Physical being pretty

Thought she was a hustler

So she gamble with her life

Rolled the dice

Fucked for the Ice

Stayed nice

Said "To hell with the preacher man's advice!"

Sexual gratification was the price

For his advice

That's why he always tried to entice her into his church

Where the preacher man does his unholy work

But she was now free of his satanic grip

But still deeply enslaved

Due to her western ways

She developed a scheme of getting rich

With her older fastidious lesbian Bitch

Who convinced her to love Pussy more than Dick

Found themselves in a combination of shit

When they tried to rob Big Mike for his ghetto treasures

But the consequences they didn't measure

Now the streets became even more difficult and complex

Lesbian companion found slain in a Lex

Purchased with Big Mike's Gs

Found her self snorting raw dope out of his keys

To suppress and neutralize her pain

Visions of bloody bodies

Pushing her to the brink of becoming insane

Purchased a .380

Found out that she was pregnant with Big Mike's baby

Tried to make a run for the border with her brand new daughter

But ran out of cash

Wind up selling infected ass

For barely enough money to cop a blast

Her life was slipping and fading fast

Wind up running back to Big Mike

To try to make things right

But was rejected

No longer respected

Or sorted after sexually

Mike no longer desired to kill her for her treachery

She was a pitiful sight for him to see

Wind up given her a blast for free

That burst her veins

And ended her pain

Returned her to the place where her innocence remains

Revolution! Created by: Heru Senghor

Fatherless Child Part I

Wild fatherless child

Stepped off the steps into the ghetto confusion

Was sick of his mother illusions

Liquor abusing

So he decided to take his chances on the streets

Stomach was hungry so he had to eat

Shit wasn't easy bitches treated him greasy

He snorted protection

Fatherly affection

So he joined a gang

Started to sling them things

Got shot in a robbery attempt one night in the rain

Bitch ass niggas he was hanging with didn't feel his pain

Left him to die in the rain

Woke up in a hospital bed

Preacher man standing by his side

Told him his Mom was no longer alive

She committed suicide

Couldn't stand losing another man

No tears rolled out of his eyes

Only the strong survive

Silently ran through his head

As he contemplated killing the Niggas that confined him to the hospital bed

Thought he was Tupac and Biggie combined

Seen the niggas who shot him and threw up a gang sign

While releasing shots at the same time

Got away clean with the crime

Started spending quality time with his lady

Nine months later she delivered his baby

He had the cash and ghetto fame

He promised his baby she wouldn't experience his pain

But he was still stuck in the game

He wanted to protect and respect his daughter

And give her the father he never had

But he still couldn't define Dad

Did something he hadn't anticipated

Asked a Yoruba priest for advice

"If you love your daughter

You have to sacrifice your life for her survival

Be a man

Understand that her future is in your hands

Teach her to be strong

And she will have the power to raise a nation

Prepare her for the struggle that she will soon be facing"

I understand

Step out the door with a newfound vision

Decided it was time to make that decision

To get out of the game

All of a sudden he felt a burst of pain

He began to contemplate about his Momma's suicide

If only he would have stayed

She would still be alive

That night he cried uncontrollable tears

He vowed to change his life around

But Ma'at was approaching as he stepped out of his car

He was grabbed from behind

As a sharp blade danced smoothly across his throat

He saw his daughter crying and a lonely woman holding a fatherless child

Revolution! Created by: Heru Senghor

My Pain

My pain exists in this burning abyss

I can't control my rage

Young, Black and locked in this cage

Growing old with the length of the days

My soul is crushed

I feel like Rosa Parks at the back of the bus

I'm about to spontaneously combust

Make me want to holler

Louder than Ja-Rule

Marvin Gaye

And Nathan McCall

But who still believe in me enough

To heed the call?

They want all young Black prisoners on death row so they can murder us all

I'm trapped in the circle of death

Struggling to hold on to my last breath

Hell is where I'm at

Bodies are always falling before my eyes

Around my way nobody is scared to die

We welcome death

Its just another form of theft

When some brother plays the role of Grim Reaper and steals your breath

I'm tired of dying

I want to live

But I feel like that little Black Boy with that bullet in his head

Everybody is pointing the finger at me

Although I've been dead for four centuries

Why don't you understand?

My tears of blood are not because I'm a Thug

It is a result of my lack of love

Give me a 9mm and sixteen slugs

And watch how fast I shed our enemies blood

We can't continue to be passive and weak

I don't need nobody to preach to me about oppression

I'm a living example of that lesson

Preacher, I'm no longer waiting on Jerusalem slim

I am him and he is me

The one who rose above the six layers

The answer to your prayers

So stop blaming me

I'm your liberty

You are going to pay for what you done

Disrespecting Ra-Amon

No matter what you do to us we are still the children of the Sun

Go ahead and have your fun

Because your days are shortening by the minute

Where are our ancestors?

They fought for our survival

But they are still not recognized

Because they are not displayed in the Bible or Qur'an

I rather sing a Yoruba hymn then a unholy A'dhan

But I'm in no mans land

Sinking in the evil Arabian

Somebody grab my hand

And pull me out of this desolate land

It ain't peaches and cream

We will never attain the American dream

I'm tired of being a slave

I'm ready to be released

So you can call me a hater for becoming a Dragon slayer

Billy D. should have killed that Bitch Princess Leia

I can feel the steam from the Dragon's nostrils

As he calls me a Nigga and lets loose his flames

As our women quietly watched us suffer in pain

I rose above the flames

But I'm still engulfed in the smoke

Uncover your ears so you can hear me choke

And know that my pain exist in this burning abyss

Revolution! Created by: Heru Senghor

A Freak In The Jail House

A freak in the jail house, not a homosexual

But sometimes I wonder

Is a man fucking a man

Synonymous to a man fucking himself with his own hand

An addiction that makes me harder than Min

Thinking about my sisters and all the positions I can put them in

Is this stress that makes me visualize visions of non-consensual sex

While I grab, pull and squeeze until I'm weak in the knees

I'm never at ease after I complete this act

I feel like a rapist and vow to never come back

But I never stick to that

Once my body gets to calling

I ask for a magazine and plenty of vaseline

While my seeds shout and scream

From the choking and the stroking

I'm hoping I can be forgiven

For the execution that I'm giving

To my unborn children

Sacrificing their life for an animal-like feeling

A false sexual healing

I cant describe the shame

The unbearable aching pain

Say my name, say my name

How can I kick the habit

When I want to fuck like bunny rabbits

Savage

Beyond sick

Skin peeling off of my dick

I need discipline to regain control

All the lust pruned out of my soul

This should be every righteous revolutionary's goal

We can't salute the people with a clenched dick

Power to the people

Revolution! Created by: Heru Senghor

Adoration To Nut

My emotional devotion is expressed through this lyrical potion

Telepathic thoughts

Enter into your heart

Your body excites

The words that I write

I hold your picture at night

As I travel through the universe and star gaze

Like two eagles performing a mating rite

I hover above the stars at night

Watching you through the twilight

Battling through an astrological storm of meteorites

Just to keep our cosmology tight

As your womb expands both day and night

Giving birth to the Sun in the morning and swallowing him back up at night

Intergalactically I pause . . .

Stuck in between Earth and Mars

Face to face with a constellation of stars

Phoenix appeared amongst the stars

As I descend She rises

With heat in her eyes

I taste the fire between her thighs and become immortal

As I escape through her portal

She spits me out of her womb

I have diamonds in my eyes

As I separate the Earth from the sky

My melanin shakes and shifts in my bones

Whenever I imagine us being alone

Somewhere distant

Deep as the quasars

Giving birth to the Stars

Revolution! Created by: Heru Senghor

Was My Love Lust Or True

I loved her with all my young might

She was the first immaculate women I ever had

I kind of regret opening her up and spreading her legs

But we were too young to understand

That this wasn't proper behavior for a young Black women and a young Black man

This was our Ghetto drama

Or should I say our ghetto trauma

That made me hated and despised by her momma

But I was on cloud 9

Thought I was living, but I was actually dying

Caught up in an illusion

Was my love lust or confusion?

She made me feel liberated and elated

An ignorant mind

I was driven in the blind

And she helped me see

That there was something unique and special about me

By giving me her love

While everybody else considered me a worthless Thug

We always craved for our flesh to be intertwined

Her powerful juices soaking the roots of my tree

Was this love?

Lust?

Or an escape that we used

To step away from the ghetto blues

Or the family dissent

That made us emotionally deprived

I swear if it wasn't for her love I might not have survived

In a world of lies and daily death

She gave me life and hope for the future

I wanted her to always be mine

She kept the tears from falling when I was in deep pain

Her body was Golden Brown and glowed in the dark

I was excited when she invited me inside her warmth

The energy I received from her body made me feel like a celestial being

She kissed my pain away when I was jumped on by Western District goons

Crazed-cops, killers who inflicted deep wounds

As if I was a slave rebellious to their system

Therefore worthy of death

She embraced me in her arms and revitalized me with her breath of life

She was too young to comfort me throughout the night

But I could see it in her eyes

I could taste it in her kisses

I could hear it in her moans

I could feel the vibration all through her bones

That she didn't want to leave my side

Nor did I want her to leave my side

With her legs wrapped tightly around my thighs

Visualizing us going half on a baby

Was this love?

Lust?

Or two young people who went crazy

Imagine a 16yr old boy trying to impregnate a 15yr old girl

Thinking this will bring more love and happiness into our world

But I didn't succeed

Lucky for me and her

Because I was deeply enslaved

Our baby would have went straight from the cradle into the grave

As time went by my environment eventually swallowed me up

It was like rehab

Because her body and love I had to have

Our separation gave me the shakes

Felt like I was bitten by poisonous snakes

Sweating hard as my body continued to ache

I could no longer touch her

I could no longer caress her

I could no longer hear her voice whispering I love you in my ear

I no longer had her to bring happiness into my microcosm

To prevent my tears from drowning me in sorrow

I no longer had my hope for tomorrow

Was my love lust or true?

Revolution! Created by: Heru Senghor

The Whiteman Got My Woman

The Whiteman got my woman and I don't understand the connection

How could she show affection

To the man that raped her of her sacredness?

Castrated her fathers and sold her children at the auction block

I stop

I think

I contemplate

And I wait . . .

For an answer

And she just stands there staring me blindly in my face with her beautiful eyes . . .

And hunches her shoulders to my despise

She sashayed down the walk and I said

Sister! Sister! Please!

Give me some insight because I truly don't understand

What in the hell you see in this diabolical white man?

I stop

I think

I contemplate

And I wait for an answer . . .

And she just stands there staring me blindly in my face with her beautiful eyes . . .

And puts her hand on her hip and twists her lip to my despise

She sashayed down the walk and I said

Sister! Sister! Please!

Help me understand

What would make you lay in the sack with such a beast of a man?

I stop

I think

I contemplate

And I wait . . . for an answer

And she just stands there staring me blindly in my face with her beautiful eyes . . .

And turns her back to my despise

She sashayed down the walkway and I said

Sister! Sister! Please!

Explain to me how could you kiss him without tasting our Ancestors blood on his fangs?

I stop

I think

I contemplate

And I wait . . . for an answer

And she stands there staring me blindly in my face with her
beautiful eyes . . .

And she rolled her eyes to my despise

She sashayed down the walkway and I say

Sister! Sister! Please!

I really want to know

What possessed you to allow this demon to capture your soul?

I stop

I think

I contemplate

And I wait . . . for an answer

And she stands there staring me blindly in my face with her
beautiful eyes . . .

And sucked her teeth to my despise

She sashayed down the walkway and I say

Sister! Sister! Please!

I am trying to comprehend

How could you allow his scaly hand to caress the soft bosom
of your breast?

I stop

I think

I contemplate

And I wait . . . for an answer

And she just stood there staring me blindly in my face

with a trickle of a tear running down her beautiful eyes

She turned to me and said . . .

Because you abandoned me Brother and a part of me died

You left me with our kids and bills I couldn't possibly pay on my own

You got me put out of my house while you slept in my best friends home

Beat me when I wanted to cuddle

Disrespected me when all I wanted was a little respect

You made me dependent on the White man and his welfare check

Of course I'd rather have you Black man

But you are the Whiteman is disguise

Yes you, Black Brother

To my despise

Revolution! Created by: Heru Senghor

Respecting Our Women

Respecting our women is not an obligation but a natural inclination

Without her we would be unable to germinate our seeds

We learn in our African Society that she is the first teacher

She nurtures our young

The honorable Elijah Muhammad teaches us that she is reflection of the Sun

She is to be revered like Ra-Amon

She brings forth our prophets and liberators

Her role in our life is vast and major

Without her transforming power we wouldn't last

She fought many battles to keep us free

When we was blind she help us see the signs

I speak of a Dr. Francis Cress Welsing type mind

Our women possess

I must confess

Our women are Diviners

If we would have only listened to their precognition we wouldn't be suffering here in perdition

Clean that wax out of your ears

Turn that hip-hop down and listen!

Stop degrading our women

If it wasn't for her you wouldn't even be around

Do I have to remind you of Harriet Tubman and the many lives she saved?

Through the Underground Rail to keep you from being Enslaved

I can imagine all our strong women turning over in their graves

We have to respect our women and return to our ancient ways

Before we were westernized and made into slaves

And develop our oppressors trifling disrespectful ways toward women

This thing emanates from this very beginning

It's time to focus on bigger things than sinning

Like protecting and respecting our Black women

Caring for her is respecting her to the highest degree

She spread her wings to set us free

In times of crisis she gave her life for me

You

The collective whole

It's because of her we still possess a soul

You remember the story of Queen Nzinga I told

The African women who was Courageous and Bold

Nzinga! Nzinga! Nzinga!

Spirit resides in all women

And our ancestors knew this from the very beginning

That's why they respected our Black women

They knew her powerful force and role as creator

That's why they would never degrade her

Look at our women in the eyes

Her beauty is enough to make you cry

This is one of the many reasons we should respect her until the day we die

Respecting!

Respecting!

Respecting our women!

Revolution! Created by Heru Senghor

She Jazzed Me

She was like a summer breeze

She put my mind at ease

I thought she was just a tease

When she came around I could hardly breathe

My nose was wide open

And I was hoping

To play her a melody

And to my surprise she fell for me

Her walk was full of fire

Her eyes burned deep with passion

Our body had a electromagnetic attraction

There was Jazzz between us

And she was playing the sweetest melody

Her obsession grabbed ahold of me

My heart was pounding

As the music increased under the light of the stars

We made looove . . . to the rhythm of the universe

Time had completely stop

As we rocked the Earth off its axis

I could hear the soothing melodies of the saxophone

Each time she moaned

Her body glowed in the moonlight

The music played all night

This was Jazzz

This was Jazzz

She jazzed me and I can still hear her sweet melodies playing in the rhythm of my heartbeat

She was sweet

Purple black

Beautiful strong

And she Jazzed me

All night long

We continue to jam and travel through space and time

She gave me more than sex

She gave me her mind

Body

And soul

Our love was whole and hot

Like a ray of sun

We became one with the earth

I planted seeds

As the music transformed into soft silent screams of pleasure

We danced

And our love making enhanced

Into spiritual chants

A ritualistic romance

And the saxophone continues to play

Until the break of day

When the sun did rise

I opened my eyes

And she was gone

It couldn't have been a dream

Because I could still feel the steam

Heat

And rhythm of her love

This was Jazzz

This was Jazzz

She Jazzed me and I can still hear her sweet melodies playing in the rhythm of my heartbeat

She was sweet

Purple black

Beautiful strong

And she jazzed me

All night long

Revolution! Created by: Heru Senghor

Thinking Of You

My thoughts of you keep us connected

But I am still affected

By our physical separation

I miss embracing

Tasting

Your chocolate kisses

Spontaneous actions

Burning passion

Nineteen years

Of blood

Sweat

And tears

Fears

But we are still here

Going strong

I remember when you tried to stop me from doing wrong

Knew the life style that I was living was doing more harm than good

But I was hungry for the papers

Another day another caper

I wanted to stop

Especially after I was maliciously beaten by the cops

But I was addicted to drugs

Surrounded by thugs

And they got the best of me

And I know I was wrong for giving you the rest of me

You gave me the greatest gift in the world

A beautiful little girl

That one day we will raise together

I will love you and my child forever

I am all smiles

As I think about how we use to be buck-wild

Remember Miami Beach

You was hot

And it wasn't because of the heat

That night our love making was sweet

I saw the Sun

Moon

And Stars in your eyes

And it makes me want to cry

That I can't reach out and touch you

Stretch you

To your limit

Electromagnetic

Static

I am addict

For your love

I am gravitating

Closer and closer to you with my thoughts

Can't you feel my heart beating

Beat

Beating

Me heavily breathing

As I kiss your neck

I am giving you more than sex

I am giving you my soul

I will be thinking of you until I physically depart from Earth

And then I will watch you from the sky

My thoughts of you keep me alive

Revolution! Created by: Heru Senghor

Soul Mates

I found in my lifetime what some will never find

A woman deeply connected to my spirit

Body

And Mind

Although our physical is suspended in time

Our love continues to Bump and Grind

Each time

We find each other in our thoughts

Our hearts become one

A passion that burns hotter than the Sun

I was young and didn't know how to treat her

Even cheated her out of my loyalty

When my body was in control of my spirituality

Sex became my only reality

A formality

For a young Black Ghetto child

I smile

When I think about how

She took me beyond sex

Taught me how to respect

A black woman for her intellect

We traveled to places I have never seen

She allowed me into her Universe and I discovered a heart of gold

And I long to hold

Her in my arms again

She is the Sun that makes my world spin

I wish that I could make love to her again

Although our sexual encounters didn't involve gymnastics

She was fantastic

Her juices over flowed like the Nile

She wasn't that wild

When she Jazzed me

But she still managed to grab me

And kiss my inner spirit

We made love so hard that our ancestors could even hear the love chants as

We glanced in each others eyes

I saw the woman that I want to grow old with and die

I give this woman praise with her, I saw my happiest days

Our love was more than just a phase

It was full grown

In her I found a home

A place of refuge

A constant source of encouragement

Our time together was peace

A woman of eloquence and grace

She kept a smile on my face

I can still taste

Her sweet juices on my tongue

I was sprung

And our relationship had just begun

But I knew a new day was coming with the rise of Hapi

And that we would become one and from one we would become three

She is the divine representation of my authority

She crowned me with her lover

My heart sits on her eternal throne

I know that it has to be destiny and fate

Because it was written in the stars that my Brown Sugar is my Soul Mate

Revolution! Created by: Heru Senghor

Brown Sugar

I once had a girl who was as sweet as Brown Sugar

Until I decided to pick up the gun

Catch a murder charge and go on the run

She was still there

Although it wasn't fair

I thought that she would follow me anywhere

But I was young and beyond naïve

And getting caught by Five-O, I couldn't conceive

I once had a girl who was sweet as Brown Sugar

Until I became a statistic

Another black male locked in a jail cell

She wrote me letters and came to see me as often as she could

I was still innocent until proven guilty

But things were looking good

We used to talk on the phone

Tripping and reminiscing about all the past times we were missing

I once had a girl that was as sweet as Brown Sugar

Until I received my sentence

15yrs for lack of repentance

My transition from jail to prison was an interesting one

That's when I first start to realize I was child of the Sun

My Brown Sugar letters became less and less

And every phone conversation we had was practically nonexistent

Or an out-and-out mess

I told her she possessed the spirit of Queen Nzinga

Hatshepsut

And Tiye

That she is the mother of civilization and the teacher of the rest

I told her that she was the first

The original

And there for the best

But she labeled me another Black fool

Who went to prison and eat all the wrong food

I once had a girl who was as sweet as Brown Sugar

Until I evolved from my boyhood stage and started directing my Black rage

Toward the Puppet Master

The Unseen Hand

The perpetual enemy of the Black man

I lost my Brown Sugar because she couldn't choose

Between the resurrected Hannibal or that old Negro fool

I am still traumatized over the fact

Of losing the beauty I ever seen in Black

I once had a girl who was as sweet as Brown Sugar

Revolution! Created by: Heru Senghor

Midnight

Midnight

The shadow of Sunlight

Creeping into my thoughts at night

Concealed in your darkness is the ultimate light

Body airtight

Mind instrumental to the struggle

When you walk the earthquakes

And our enemies try to escape

Your solar eclipse and the powerful words released from your full lips

Dangerous and deadly by design

Rather carry a gun than a picket sign

Of the same mind and spirit of Sister Assata Shakur

Ain't standing behind no man

But next to him

Armed in the struggle hand and hand

Only the righteous qualified to be her man

Some Brothers still don't understand

The Blacker the berry the sweeter the juice

And I am trying to dig down deep into your African roots

To reproduce the mind and spirit of Cetewayo

And I wont stop until you exhale

I got to get a woman in your image and likeness

And I hope you understand why I am writing this

If not

Its because you have a beautiful spirit and a Milk Chocolate body

And your letters have done nothing but inspired me

To try to set my mind free

You are as sweet as a Hershey Kiss

And even a fool can see

In my darkest hour I can depend on Midnight to comfort me

Revolution! Created by: Heru Senghor

Sunshine

Sunshine has healed my pain

Brought an end to the rain

Burst through the gray sky

No longer will I cry

About a lost love

Because I can hear the birds sing in the spring

When Sunshine turns the vegetation green

In the summer breeze

Sunshine shines her rays through the trees

And wraps her rays tightly around me

Sunshine, beautiful and disrobed

Too much heat for any man to stay in control

It only takes her eight minutes and twenty seconds to completely subdue a man

Sunshine came in the middle of the winter many years ago

And bust her ass in the snow

After that she clung to me and never let go

Although she's 93 million miles away

Her burning passion reaches me everyday

Man has been in love with sunshine since the beginning of time

Her body is a sacred shrine

To kiss the Sun would be divine

Every time I am in the Sun, chills run through my spine

Because I can feel the Sunshine absorbing into my skin

Making me hot

Sweaty

Hard and ready

To penetrate the seeds to help Sunshine bring about new life

Sparkling red

If I could, I would take Sunshine to bed

Use her warmth as a soft pillow for my head

Her fervent body I would unite with mine

So we could become one Hot Burning Ball Of Sunshine

Revolution! Created by: Heru Senghor

I Miss You

I can't believe its been so many years since I saw your beautiful face

Or felt your warm and loving tender embrace

Sometimes I look for you in the stars deep in outer space

Wondering where you're at

And if you can feel my energy

Stretching out my hands in an attempt to feel you

But you're not there

Confusing your body presence with the warmth of summers air

Its not fair

You being with him and me being all alone

Missing you

Wishing I was home

To treat you like the Queen that you are

I would take you away from him

To a place of Holy Matrimony

And we would live happily ever after

In rapture

I would capture the essence of your beauty

By exploring your mind

But I wouldn't leave your body behind

Because I know its dying

To feel the gentle but rough touch of a real man's hand

I remember every curve

How you like your belly button kissed

And how you would twist

When my tongue slid between your legs

You would grab my head and push

Gasping for air

As we lay there in love and satisfaction

Thinking of you makes me erotic

Your body is hypnotic

Your smile is captivating

And I hope you're still waiting

Because I miss your love

And it won't be long now

Before I am able to drown

You with my kisses

And shower you with my hugs

Creating an atmosphere where your child would experience
true fatherly love

And hopefully we can drop a seed of our own

I hope you'll still be there for me when I come home

I miss you!

Revolution! Created by: Heru Senghor

The Things We Forgot

The things we forgot

Can be found written in MDW NTR on the pyramid blocks

Chambers we unlock

And explore African culture we adore

Visualizing sisters with children on their backs

With African head wraps

Hands clap

Stomping feet

To the sound of the African drum beats

The sun's heat

Keeps our melanin intact . . . and in tune with the earth

As it gives new birth

Crops springing forth from the soil

For we worked hard and toiled

To bring forth civilizations

And all forms of education, philosophy, mathematics, religion and science

One with the Creator for we formed an alliance . . .

As we look towards the Old Lady and the seven stars for guidance

We break the seal that reveals the coming forth by day

We pray and follow Molefe Asante, The way . . .

The way of Old

Blessed with the land that possesses old, silver, diamonds, oil and rubies

Raising our children and protecting our women are our moral duties

The life we lived was a life to give

And contribute to the universal balance

Now we're confronted with this new challenge

To restore all that was great

Mentally elevate

Beyond our physical state

And transverse the sky

So we can rebuild our community through African eyes

Struck with Zeal

As I asked the council of elders to help me to appeal

To the hearts of men

To re-instill Ma'at again

The beginning that has no end

Emerged in Ptahhotep's creative words

Native doctors curing our ills with their holistic herbs

African masks and sculptures

Helps us express our beautiful culture

Bring light to the glory of our land

The heat in the Sahara sands

Black & Beautiful like the original man

On top like Kilimanjarooooo . . .

Ancestors whisperrrrr in the winnnnnd . . .

Listen to us again

It's not a sin

To find honor and value in

Our ancestral kin

Whose accomplishments transcend

The boundaries of time

Only if you appreciate and remember them in the confinement of your mind

Remember, Remember, Remember . . .

When Queen Candice stood her ground

And chumped Alexander the so-called Great down

And Imhotep whose knowledge was profound

Build pyramids when other traces of civilizations couldn't be found

Blood is old

It doesn't change

Our Ancestor's blood flow through our veins

Ra's creative force exists in all things

The sun, moon, stars and even the air that we breathe

Trees, grass, dirt and the ocean seas

This is what our Ancestors believed

Don't be deceived

By the lying distortions of his-story

Look at our past and you'll see that there is glory

There is greatness

There is pride

When looking at Africa

Don't just see Apartheid

Don't just see civil strife, starvation and A.I.D.S.

See beautiful Black women with their hair plaited in braids

See strong Black men who will fight for their fertile land

The potential to expand

Don't see heathens, savages, pagans, and mutilators

See healers, scientists, builders and educators . . .

So please Blackman

Take our hand

Let's take that stand

And start this journey

Our souls are yearning

For accurate representations and immaculate manifestations
of . . .

The things we forgot

The things we forgot

Revolution! Created by: Heru Senghor & Imhotep 7 aka Elo

Destruction Of Black Civilization

I have it all in one place

Destruction of Black Civilization is the reason why we are in this backward state

Need I remind you of what took place in this land

Just take a look at the soil and you'll understand

See the resemblance of the Blood of the Blackman

Woman and child

The murder rate was high

And is still at a maximum level

Every since we were kidnapped

Debased

And dehumanized by the devil

You still come at me with religious nonsense

Talking about it ain't all about being Black

You lucky Ausar doesn't get Ra to burn you alive for saying something like that

For what you say is wrong

We're The Children of the Sun and that's what makes us strong

In time of need we seek refuge in Amon

For he knows the most strategic way of breaking the chains

Once He enters into our minds and hearts we can do all things

So why should I submit to a religion that's not even yours

When the only thing its good for is conquering people in psychological wars

Patriotic American Negro Fool

You're sick in the head

Won't even venerate our ancestors who gave their lives for you

Talking about these are the things your religion tells you not to do

While their screams continue to echo in the wind

You cover your ears and pretend not to hear

Your chastisement will be immense and serve

Which I will personally deliver for the Gods

Revolution!

Revolution!

And no more preaching hard!

Revolution! Created by: Heru Senghor

Death

Everybody dreads the day when we receive death

Close our eyes and take our last breath

Who knows where our fallen soldiers lie

Do they return to the earth

Or some mythological place in the sky

Is there a God who judges us on this day of death

Who explains to us why our life was such a wretched mess

Then sentences us to another hell

Because he say we didn't give him proper praise

Totally neglecting the fact that he's the one who allowed us to be enslaved

We will be stuck in suspended animation

Or will we soak in the soil of the earth

Evolve into a flower or tree when Ra strikes us with His powerful rays

And water from the rain feeds us nutrition for days

Or do we live through posterity

Because their blood is ours

Look at the young brother as he lie wounded in the streets

Riddled with bullet holes as he enters into eternal sleep

He's shaking

He is trying to fight it

But its useless

The day he dreaded has come

His eyes are closing

His last breath roams through the earth with the wind

He knows the answer to all our questions

As the darkness of death overcomes Him

Revolution! Created by: Heru Senghor

My Life

My life

My life

My life is never Sunshine

Why are you punishing me

Just when I start to taste what its like to be free

You snatch my life away from me

Why can't I be the chosen one

I represent Ra-Amon

Geb

And ain't I a member of the children of The Sun

Jehewty I am not ready for my heart to be weighed on the scales of Ma'at

And I openly confess this

I am just starting to understand my Jet in relation to my Ba

But I don't know it intimately enough for my heart to be weighed on the scales of Ma'at

And I openly confess this

I am just starting to understand my Jet in relation to my Ba

But I don't know it intimately enough to reunite it with my Ka

If I were to become deceased

It wouldn't be in hotep

It would be in dismay

Because I haven't planted any seeds in the Earth to replace my birth

There's nothing I would like more then to become an eternal spirit and come forth by day

But I must say

I wasn't allowed to spread my wings physically

And now you want me to spread them metaphysically

My life

My life

My life is never Sunshine

I am tired of dying

Send me an Egungun so I can plead my case

My whole life has been maligned and debased

I wish I could talk to you Face to Face

I am man enough not to request that anyone take my place

My family is not a family because of our disorientation

When I die who is going to stand up to protect the Black Nation

I put you in front of all the rest

Now I request that you show me your best

Cure me if need be

Give me knowledge

Help me to become a walking Black college

My belief and Imani is solid

I've seen your works

My pain is deep

I am just waking up

And now you want to put me to sleep

Why can I no longer feel the rays of Ra's heat

My days are becoming longer and at night I refuse to sleep

But I still continue to strive

Although these may be the last days of

My life

My life

My life is never Sunshine

Revolution! Created by: Heru Senghor

Your Spirit Reigns

What pains

As the image remain clear

Thoughts I hold dear

Of the time when you were here

I refuse to become bitter now that you are gone

I'll be strong and carry on

Facing life obstacles in every conceivable way

Every time I pray

I mention your name

No pain

Just love

You departed physically from the Earth

But your soul still traveling with the stars

Rising with the Sun

And you will be missed simple and plain

As we face this mundane world

We'll hold tight to your memories of days gone by

Although we question why

He had to take you away

I know everybody has there time

I just wish he would have gave you a fraction of mine

I'm crying

Tears of libation for God's primordial creation

Who touch so many lives

We know the eternal spirit never dies

It only returns from which it came

And in God's Kingdom your spirit reigns

Revolution! Created by: Heru Senghor and Taharka Senghor

Becoming An Ancestor

I look toward the sky at night

And I see the twinkling of starlight

Casting my problems to the primordial Father in the moonlight

Searching for Ma'at in the expanding universe

I feel cursed

Anchored in the Earth

Restrained

Trying to transcend from my earthly domain

And become an astral projection

Part of Ma'at's perfection

I step outside of my body each time

My sunsum takes over my conscious mind

I am inclined

To look for answers in the cosmological order

I drink from the Old Lady's water

My mind elevates

And my body levitates

My soul is released through my chest cavity

Escaping gravity

Until I awake . . .

Trapped in the same mundane body

Facing the same mundane fate

It aches

The thought of being reincarnated

Having my soul reinstated

In the same dust of the Earth

That blows to and fro with the wind

Facing the same trails and tribulations all over again

I want to be an eagle and sore in the wind

I want to reunite the Earth with the sky

Because one with out the other will surely die

My eyes reflect the light of the Sun and the Moon

And one day soon

I will rise

But not before my time

Preparations must be made

Before I return to my earthly grave

And embrace my spiritual Mother

I must discover

The path that has been preordained

And laid

Before my heart is weighed

So that it will be as light as a feather

And so my name can live forever

In the hearts and minds of my people

Who will rejoice and sing

Remembering their Ancestor

Who accomplished extraordinary things

Revolution! Created by: Heru Senghor

Untitled

Its 2000 and we are still waiting on a miracle

A sign from something divine

In stead of using our minds

Your searching for something you'll never find

Because you're looking in all the wrong places

Ra has many faces

He is the light that shines internally bright

With in your minds you are divine

Feel the energy from your own divinity

The Blackman

Woman

And child is the holy trinity

The most powerful entity

Blessed and endowed with the blood substance of the Creator

The originators

Of the planetary system

We don't need a miracle to succeed

When the air that we breathe

Is the breath of Auset

That gives us the power to build

Create

And wake others up

To see the eye of Ra on the horizon

Black people no longer dying

Because they hear the drums

Beating

Beat

Beating

Heavily

Deep in their souls

Unleashing the rhythm that puts us back in control

Of our own thinking

2000 got to be Black

Roy Ayers taught us that

Waiting on a miracle prevents us from seeing that

What we need can be found in pure black

Close your eyes and visualize that

Revolution! Created by: Heru Senghor

The Apocalypse

Blind vision

The stillness of the night

Rain coming down nonstop it turns to blood

Screams echoing in the wind

Trees ripped from their foundation

Oceans desiccated because of the misunderstanding it has with the sun

Stars rebelling against the moon

Black holes are forming with the promise of Doom

Revolution! Created by: Heru Senghor

The Rhythm Is Life

The rhythm is life and the life is rhythm

They got me trapped in a cage

Surrounded by Black rage

Because I refuse to consummate with the devil or submit to his ways

I keep moving like the primeval waters

Bow down only to the original Gods

The ennead ones who created the sun and the length of the days

The Gods that will never allow us to be enslaved

Changed your filthy diabolical ways

Listen to the Rhythm . . .

Because the Rhythm is Life and Life is Rhythm

I am the catalyst who started it all

Who allows Atum to sit on the Hill

Through the rhythm of my words

I created all that I conceived in my heart

Will and intent is the key to your focus

Lose sight of this and wind up like your enemies struck with psychoneurosis

The Rhythm of your thoughts is your arch

So don't lose control

You're the only one that knows the power your cerebral holds

Listen to the Rhythm . . .

Because The Rhythm is life and The Life is Rhythm

My mutant offspring's mad at me for not giving them what they desire

The Rhythm to move like me . . .

Melanin inspired

Their pale

Red

Flaccid body's craving for the Rhythm

Something that Ra will never ever give them

They were born albinos and then evolved into ghostly Devils

Prone to murder

Mayhem and trouble

Try to snuff out your brain

Because of their alienation

Anxiety

Narcissism and pain

Listen to The Rhythm so you can know these things

The Rhythm is Life and The Life is Rhythm

Its time to break free from your mental prison

Valtron was the Bomb

Consolidate and the enemy can do you know harm

The Great Ancestor sees all that you do

So just listen to The Rhythmmm

And He will manifest Himself in you

Because The Rhythm is Life and Life is Rhythm

Revolution! Created by: Heru Senghor

Come Back To Reality

Intergalactic travel

You niggas babble on

Like Babylon your reign won't last long

Mentally drown to the wrong sources of energy

Wires crossed

Lost in space

Trying to save face

So you created the extraterrestrial Meldeckin race

Meanwhile

Back on earth Brothers continue to fall by the wayside

Waiting on the Mothership to arrive

How many more will die

Before we realize the answer to our problems are not going to fall out of the sky

Pure insanity

I am part of Hue-manity

Who the Fuck came up with the idea of a Black Guerrilla Family

Maybe that's why our neighborhoods are jungles and we only heed to the call of the wild

Niggas are foul

Predators on the prowl

Locked down behind cages

Trying to understand the different stages of Man

From Blood

Bone

And Flesh

To our metaphysical existence

I stand alone

A strong link

In a broken chain

Repressing pain

Just so that I can make it through the day

I pray

For those Brothers who consciously choose to remain to be grimy

Justice is real

And in the court of Ma'at they are no appeals

I hope that you are ready to receive your Just reward

Because those who live by the sword die by the sword

Bones shaking in religious fanatics worse than addicts

When they discover that they have been living a lie

There is no sweet pastry waiting for them in the sky

I knew all along

That we existed before protoplasm and even the first Atum
(Adam, Atom)

Because in the beginning there was only one

Ptah creative energy in the form of Atum

Who gave birth to the Neteru who gave birth to everyone

So you're more than extraterrestrial your celestial

So stop functioning off of your Beastly testicles

You can't prove me wrong

I been around for too damn long for your computers to
calculate a date

You still don't understand

I am the primordial Blackman

I know my origins don't lie in no geographical land

But my vehicle is made up of the best part of the Earth

Alkebulan dirt

So don't try to downplay my physical existence

It has its role

It's the only conduit for the soul

Protects me from the ultraviolet rays of the Sun

And keeps me in tune with the creation of Amen

What happen to the Walking Talking Language

Vocal cords got strangled

When the Blackman got tangled

In a geometric shape worst than the Bermuda Triangle

While other Brothers wait

For others to dictate their fate

I escape to the land of the Blacks

My original habitat

And send a message in a bottle for other Brothers and Sisters to come back to life

Come Back to Reality

Revolution! Created by: Heru Senghor